If I Try To Be Like Him,

Who Will Be Like Me?

אַז איך וועל זײַן ווי ער,

ווער וועט זײַן ווי איך?

If I try to be like him,

who will be like me?

Ahz ich vel zayn vee er,

ver vet zayn vee ich?

(Calligraphic hand of Jay Greenspan, in Yiddish
and English transliteration, from the epigraph
of the author's earlier chapbook, Al Het)

If I Try To Be Like Him, Who Will Be Like Me?

Poems by

Zev Shanken

Full Court Press
Englewood Cliffs, New Jersey

Published in the United States of America
by Full Court Press, 601 Palisade Avenue,
Englewood Cliffs, NJ 07632
fullcourtpress.com

ISBN 978-1-946989-21-5
Library of Congress Catalog No. 2018958563

ALSO BY ZEV SHANKEN
Al Het
Memory Tricks

Calligraphy by Jay Greenspan
Editing and book design by Barry Sheinkopf
Cover art by the author
Cover design by Christine Finley

FOR JAY GREENSPAN

ACKNOWLEDGMENTS

Red Wheelbarrow: "Triolets," "Ellen," "In the Colonoscopy Recovery Room," "Leonard Cohen," "The Six-Day War: An American Jewish Volunteer's Notes (Israel, 1967)"

New Verse News: "Western Civ.," " Prick an American," "A Hora for the First Passover Under President Trump"

Brevitas Festival: "Cento: The Kind of Poet I Wanted To Be Was the Kind," "Erev Bah—Evening Comes"

Response: "First Visit to In-Laws," "One Month After the Six-Day War," "Israel," "Al Het"

From Somewhere to Nowhere: "I Dreamed I Fired the Family Photographer Under Trump's Influence"

The following read some or all of the poems in this book at different stages and provided encouragement: Alice Twombly, Mike Wineberg, Stephen Bluestone, Rim Meirowitz, Jackie Gutwirth, Dan Gover, and Barry Sheinkopf.

I also wish to thank the entire *brevitas* community of online poets dedicated to the short poem, and the loyal regulars who attend *Thursdays Are for Poetry* at Classic Quiche in Teaneck, New Jersey. The *TAFP* group has become a monthly "minyan" of working poets who generously and eagerly share their writing and critical skills with alacrity and panache.

Finally, I thank Leslie for the time to write. I will always miss those moments not spent together.

About the Title

Ahz Ich Vel Zayn Vee Er, Ver Vet Zayn Vee Ich?

From the time we met in the early 1970s until his death a few days before Rosh Hashanah 2017, Jay Greenspan was a dear friend and first responder. I always felt that, once he saw my first drafts, they had achieved a private blessing that gave them courage to withstand revisions.

Jay helped me select, transliterate, and translate a Yiddish proverb that served as the epigraph for an earlier chapbook of mine. Since Jay's death, I have come to value the proverb's insight into the habits, mannerisms, and values that define a loved one's presence. And absence. The proverb—*If I try to be like him, who will be like me?*—does not claim the speaker to be better, but only rightfully necessary and simply irreplaceable. In this first year of Jay's absence, I have come to understand the proverb as a lens through which to see Jay's approach to family, friends, art, identity, and Judaism. In memory of Jay I have chosen that proverb for the title of this book.

Also in memory of Jay, I have included some early poems that addressed issues that were of great concern to us when our friendship began. These old melodies are a public memorial to Jay Greenspan as a representative of our generation's struggles to develop new strategies for making life holy, a struggle that brought a number of us together as the "New York *Havera*" on New York's Upper West Side in the 1970s. These early poems are a memorial to those years and those friends whom Jay's death encouraged me to revisit. To use a piece of jargon from that era, these poems may capture the "consciousness of where our heads were at."

Of course, my personal relationship with Jay was that of a close friend, and I hope it is obvious that the poet of this book honors Jay most, not so much by the poems that mention him by name, nor the ones that address global concerns he and I shared, nor even by my using one of his favorite Yiddish proverbs as a title for this book, but rather by the other poems in this book, the poems that sprang from the permission Jay's affection gave this poet to be himself.

I am proud to dedicate this book to Jay Greeenspan, z"l. May his memory be a blessing.

Table of Contents

Old Melodies

What God Doesn't Understand

When Bad Guys Win

I'll Never Be A Great Poet

How Would The Truth Have Helped?

Because She's Beautiful

Old
Melodies

The smell of clean old silverware drawers בָּאֵר דוד.
צוּלTheir ketubah in a frame. It smells like the drawer.
וּשָׁאֵנוּ לְפָנֵין Smiles to go before I sleep וְחַיֵי־ד.
אֵנוּל...אָמְרֵלה לְהֵדָא בְּחוֹלְדָא Soon I'll call her "mom."
הַ־ו...when our son looks like her brother...לְאַנוּ
אֵנָאwhen her teeth look like her father's....כַדַת מַיָה.
are green eyes recessive?...are flat feet אפְרֵ־־ד?
לֵיכִי יְוּוֹכִיAre they wondering how I beat the draft?
I wish I were hungry יְהוּדָאִין גוּבְרִין כַהֲלְכוּת.
בְּקָרָא לְהַנְשֵׁיהוֹן וחַזֵין I really wish I were hungry.
כָסַף "Okay, one more slice of milk" לִיכִי וֹהַבְנָא וְ.
Why did I say "slice of milk" & why did no one notice?
"It's okay, mom, we can bring the cot up by ourselves".
The basement smelled like the drawer רָאִן לֵיה וַהֲוִין.
עֲבֵי אֲבוֹה בֵּין בְּכַסַף בֵּין בְּדַהַב בֵּין בְּמַכְסִין
"No thanks. We're really tired from the drive" בְּאֵן.
עָן ד־־־־ וְחַוִן I wish I were sleepy וְקִקִים כַּף.
כַסַף צְרוּף These springs are made of silverware .
וְקָנִינָא כָן וְאַחֲרֵיוּ־ד I really wish I could sleep .

Poetry: Zev Shanken
Calligraphy: Jay Greenspan

The Six-Day War:
An American Jewish Volunteer's Notes (Israel, 1967)

1. The Sand Box

Day 1: Dug trenches around the children's village.
Covered chicken coop windows so hens would lay eggs during blackouts.

Day 2: Poured concrete with hired Arabs and American volunteers
when not in bomb shelter meeting with Americans who had settled here years ago.
One woman had a *New Yorker* and asked about Edward Albee's new play.

Day 3: Filled sandboxes with dirt we'd stored in sacks on Day 1.
The war was nearly over.
Beat swords into plowshares; pour trench dirt into sandboxes.

Days 4 and 5: Returning soldiers gave impromptu battle reports in the dark
        dining hall.
The acoustics were bad and the Hebrew colloquial.
I didn't understand most of what was said.

Day 6: In the middle of a report, someone turned on the lights.
Dining hall exploded in cheers. Blackout over,
but we heard low-flying jets and felt the earth shake all night.

2. The American Dream

Saturday: David, who had settled in Israel years ago with the woman
who had asked about Edward Albee's new play, scolded their daughter
for defending Israel's actions in Quneitra. "They'd have done the same
        or worse to us,"
she said in fluent Israeli Hebrew. Her father protested. Jewish ethics!

Lessons of History!
His Hebrew sounded like an American teacher at a Hebrew-speaking
      summer camp.
His daughter sneered and left the room. He looked at me with shy
      exasperation and said, "Teenagers!"

Sunday: Over the eggplant-sorting machine, I asked David what will become of
the newly conquered territories. He smiled less shyly than yesterday and said,
"We'll form a Greater Israel."

Kibbutz 1966

Marx, Laing, Mailer, Reich,
Kerouac, Ginsberg, Whitman, Blake,
Miller—Henry and Arthur,
Berlin—Isaiah and Irving,
Dylan—Thomas and Bob,
Hemingway, Bellow, Kafka, Roth,
Kavafy, Alan Watts, the Bible,
Ber Borochov, Wittgenstein, and Aleph Daled Gordon.

When asked
        we'd gladly reply
        We love real life on kibbutz.

One Month After
The Six-Day War

Last night two soldiers
(I don't think they were drunk)
said to Lisa,
"Do you give your man your cunt?"

I turned around
half-shocked and half-pleased
that I'd understood their Hebrew.

"Thus speak Jewish soldiers?"
I asked, sing-song rabbinically.
They repeated my words to the tune
and mocked our holding hands.

I translated the exchange for Lisa.
She asked if Hebrew was hard.

Erev Bah—Evening Comes

*Transcription of memories while listening to the 1950's recording
by Theodore Bikel.*

1.

shuv ha-eder no-her—
　　Remember how Rhoda sang the words
bimvi'ot ha-k'far—
　　as if she knew their meaning?
ve'oleh ha-avak—
　　And when she spun,
mishvilei-afar—
　　how the grown-ups were grateful
ve'harchek od tzemed inbalim—
　　for the sexless safety of synagogue?
melave et meshech hatz'lalim—
　　Because she went to a famously difficult academy,
erev ba—
　　she always had to leave early
erev ba—
　　before traffic.

2.

shuv haruach lochesh—
　　Senior year she was part of the scandal
bein gidrot ganim—
　　that our uncles assured us would be forgotten
uv-tzameret ha-brosh—
　　or forgiven
kvar namot yonim—
　　by June.
v'harchek al ketef ha-gvaot —
　　Now, when she spins,

od noshkot, karnaim achronot—
     her hair, white skirt, and naked feet
erev ba—
     seem to say,
erev ba—
     "Even when you thought it possible,
erev ba—
     it wasn't.
erev ba—
     What's the difference now?
erev ba—
     What's the difference now?"

Time Machine: A Villanelle for the Jewish Center of Teaneck

Cables of eternal light
1950s TV joy
O my Jewish *Nick at Nite*

Twilight Zone is at its height
Stevenson is *adonoy*
Cables of eternal light

Edward Morrow tells it right
Israel does not destroy
O my Jewish *Nick at Nite*

Hertz's Chumash brings delight
Negroes learn from Jewish boy
Cables of eternal light

Wilma Flintstone Yiddishkeit
No one knows about Hanoi
O my Jewish *Nick at Nite*

Ever present, ever trite,
Clichés time cannot destroy
Cables of eternal light
O my Jewish *Nick at Nite*

Civilization in Three Stanzas

(To the tune of "Bella Ciao")

She learned a love song when she was little
in a language that she hardly knew.
|: *Oh, she would sing it as if she wrote it,*
and she made each word sound true.:|

One day her lover asked her a question
about the language that she hardly knew.
|: *She said, "I'll tell you when we get married,*
If this love of ours is true." :|

You'll find that couple singing their love song,
in the language that only they know—
|: *And all their children sing like their parents*
in a language that they hardly know.:|

Israel

After Allen Ginsberg's "America"

Israel, I wanted to give you all until I became nothing.
I couldn't stand my own mind; I had raised it for *leket*.
Israel, when will I end this war?
Go screw yourself with *Gush Imunim;* we Jews make bad idolaters.
I feel good. Why don't you start bothering me?
I won't write my poems 'til you haunt me again.
Israel, when will you become angelic?
When can I walk into the Super Sol and buy what I want
       by pronouncing it right?
I'm homesick for your ancient nomads.
Israel, after all it's you and I who are Jews, not the old world.
Israel, why are you delighted when I contradict myself?
Your intensity is too much for me.
You made me want to be a saint.
There must be some way to settle in peace.
Larry's in Jerusalem; I don't think he'll ever be happy—it's tragic.
Are you being tragic, or is this some form of cosmic educational device?
I'm trying to come to terms.
But I won't give up my obsessions either.
Israel, start pushing my soul. I know what I'm doing. It's dull.
Israel, I feel sentimental about the *biluim*—should I feel more?
Israel, whenever I see an eggplant I evaluate *sug alef, sug bet, ixtra.*
I was a student in Jerusalem years ago; I cut up but made lasting friends.
     One was an Englishman who read me Allen Ginsberg's "America."
     I'd been ashamed of beatniks 'til then. I listened to Dylan on
Jordan's propaganda radio. His songs were about justice, and the irony hurt.
I worked on collectives and ended proud of the land and my muscles.
My mind got made up I had to get troubled.
You should have seen me singing the *sh'ma* when I went crazy.

I still have trouble with prayer.

I had American visions and Jewish vibrations. In those days, all liberals
        were one.

Israel, I still haven't told you what you did to the soul of Zak Berkowitz
        after he returned to the States.

I'm wrestling with you.

I haven't read Hebrew in years; every word reminds me of time.

Are you going to let my emotional life be run by a language I can hardly read?

When I pray, I skip to the English and feel I'm missing too much
        to take the message seriously.

Israel, what too much am I missing?

I buy the *Jerusalem Post* from the Israeli owner of the newsstand
        in New York City. His air force dog

tags dangle from his shirt. Everybody thinks he's Puerto Rican.

I talk to him in Hebrew. Israel, is he Israel?

Israel, this is quite serious.

Israel, the idea was to become normal.

Israel, the idea was to become holy.

Israel, the idea was redemption.

Israel, is it all a waste unless we make new visions?

It's true I don't speak Hebrew well or have a good overview of our history.

I'm unholy and not very normal.

Israel, I'm putting my decadent materialistic bohemian unredeemed *sabony*

American shoulder to the wheel.

AL H.ET

Al Het

For the sin which I have committed before you
       by shaving with a blade,
And for the sin which I have committed before you
       by guitaring on the Sabbath.
For the sin which I have committed before you
       by eating milk chocolate after chicken.
And for the sin which I have committed before you
       by watching the priestly benediction.
For the sin which I have committed before you
       by eating bread instead of cake before the morning prayers.
For all these, O lord, give relief.

But for the sin of smashing open that first unconscious mind:
       That mind you made which can't tell time,
       committed to thumbs and puns and hidden oaths,
       father knows best, Machiavellian insomnia under the sheets,
          "Mommy, I can't sleep."
       Forgive that mind whose world is crushed
          when a toilet's flushed or a bottle's late.
       Forgive that mind which never forgets
          to put pencils in its mouth.
       Forgive that mind which taught the body
          how to get sick without germs.
For the sins of that mind that dreams awake,
       Grant redemption, O lord.
          Unsmash it to re-open in your time.

For the sin of finishing everything begun
       yet so many incompletes, forgive.
For the sin of remembering wrong.

For the sin of if it's worth doing it's worth doing well.
Sin of preparing planning never getting under way.
        Sin of never letting go to God knows what, forgive.

For the sin of deadlines.
        For the sin of having a boss.
        For the sin of needing one.
For the sin of needing Babylon in order to love Jerusalem, forgive.
        For the sin of forgetting my fathers were saints,
        For the sin of pretending my fathers were saints
                pierce my ears with the pencils from my mouth
        and only then forgive.

For the sin of not knowing where to take things seriously.
        And for the sin of asking who cares if no one cares.
For the sin of mocking therapy
        or deeming someone's madness tame, forgive.
For the sin of pop philosophy.
        Forgive the slang and quick advice—the immediate nod.
                For giving meaning to coincidence,
                        an over-read folk song. Forgive Dylanology.
Forgive another's madness when I do not forgive.

For the sin of that's true on one level but. . .
        For the sin of taking things literally.
For the sin of still not understanding
        I do do what I want.
For the sin of forgetting it can never be unlearned,
        of growing slow, misguiding your gift of forgetfulness,
                setting my mind at rest to panic for this day.
And for the sin of overeating, which dulls the mind
        and makes me feel cherubic.

Forgive the sin of sexlessness.
Forgive the book.

Forgive the dusty jacket in bed.
For digging graves I won't control, forgive.
For the sin of no, forgive.
For the sin of bankrupt fantasies.
     How old was that subway car?
     Where'd the yellow dye come from
        for this ballpoint pen?
Could it have come from some great plant
     that made the dye for yellow signs
        that tell all people going places
           to yield their right of way?
Forgive my poverty of make-believe.
Forgive sarcasm to kids.
For the sin of not liking teaching anymore, forgive.

And for the sin of no sin.
     Sometimes I feel like Bontshe Schweig in Sodom:
        New York happening everywhere and I'm still thrilled
          with home-baked bread.
              But shouldn't I be thrilled
              with home-baked bread?
     Some day I'll meet Kafka.
        He'll tell me I've always been right.
          "In every choice you made, you were right,
             only why did you waste your life?"
     Forgive the sin of that fantasy.
Forgive and grant me fear.

For the sin of humanizing your terror.
     You really have a flaming nose.
     You do have outstretched arms.
     You really truly—no metaphor—you really make the sun stand still.
     You really write down every *yud*.
Forgive me, Lord of wheels in wheels
     flaming chariots, Norden bombsights

Lord of victorious War One and Two, Six-Day War, Jericho and Ei.
You're there too.
Forgive my surprise to find you.
Bless my stupefaction.

For the sin of longing for that madness I once called only mad:
       Every thought a sign from you.
       Everything as it sounds to be.
       No imperative, only clarity.
       (Thank God I heard no voice.)
The life you gave me is not brief.
       It's going on forever.
       After death is nothing.
       This is eternity.
For the sin of abusing insomnia.

For the sin of laying this slang and heavy trip
       on a congregation of strangers, forgive.
Next time grant me private prayer.
Grant me the strength of private prayer.
Teach me what I'm saving it for.
Forgive the repetitions and the vain repetitions and help me
       accept my own repetitions and grant me the strength
          of private prayer.
You have failed me into poetry.
Show me what I'm saving it for.
Make me holy in my own design.

For the sin which I have committed before
       by shaving my nerves for no reason at all.
And for the sin which I have committed before
       by making all time as holy as your day.
For the sin which I have committed before
       by smoking poison after love.
And for the sin which I have committed before

by not becoming my own priestly benediction.
For the sin which I have committed before
  by smelling what's cooking instead of the dew before
   your morning sun.
For all these, O Lord of the universe and earthly fathers
  Lord of tradition and chains,
Lord of prophetic visions and therefore infinite variables,
  Lord of the sun and war and bed and couch
   and variations I cannot dream
Forgive, grant atonement on this day, redemption out of words,

       Amen.

In A Hospital Recovery Room I Learn
That Kenneth Koch Has Died

I remember Kenneth Koch in the balcony of the 92nd Street Y,
counting syllables at an Allen Ginsberg poetry reading.
He sat alone and moved his clean fingers like a piano player.

I knew it was Kenneth Koch because, the year before, I had sat in on his lecture
at Columbia on *Leaves of Grass* that a guy across the hall from my
room in Brooklyn was taking when he wasn't studying Chinese.

The guy and his friend were recovering addicts who played guitar well
and told me they admired me because I seemed to *have it together.*
That was the first time I heard *have it together* used like that.

At the lecture, Kenneth Koch made much of the missing period at the end of
"Song of Myself" in the Malcolm Cowley edition of the 1855 *Leaves of Grass.*
It was no accident. Whitman was a printer and typesetter.

I saw Kenneth Koch at a St. Mark's Church reading. Fans requested he read
    their favorite poem.
"This isn't a greatest hits evening." He said, "I've prepared a reading?"
That was the first time I heard a statement sung as a question like that.

I saw Kenneth Koch again with my calligrapher friend, Jay Greenspan,
at an Art Students League Symposium with Larry Rivers.
Kenneth Koch played straight man to Larry Rivers, who was insightful and silly.

Jay introduced me to David Greenstein, an artist and an orthodox
    Jewish kabbalist.
After the symposium, David took Jay and me to his East Village
    apartment to play

his father's Koussevitzky 78s. Jay explained that there were two
        famous Koussevitzkys—
Leonard Bernstein's Serge, and David Greenstein's father's generation's
        chazans: David, Jacob,
Simcha, and Moshe. When Bernstein died, I watched an interview
        where Bernstein spoke highly
of Koussevitzky, and I knew he meant Serge, not David, Jacob, Simcha,
        or Moshe.

I bought my first Kenneth Koch book, *Ko or A Season on Earth,* at a
        Brooklyn used bookstore
because I liked his use of rhyme. At the register, I hid Kenneth Koch's
        book between Jack Gelber
and Edward Field. I was afraid the Kenneth Koch would make me look square.

I bought *Thank You* on Bill Zavatsky's recommendation. Bill taught me
        how to say Kenneth
Koch's name right because he was a student at Columbia's MFA program
        and worked at
Paperback Forum and was married to a woman who had been my wife's
        roommate in college.

I bought *Rose, Where Did You Get That Red?* because David Rosenberg told
        me Kenneth Koch
understood how to teach poetry to kids and I had just landed a job
        teaching fourth graders to write
poems. Rosenberg sucked up to me because I was editor of *Response, A
        Contemporary Jewish*

Review and he had not yet become famous for *A Poet's Bible.* After my gig,
                Rosenberg met me
for coffee near NYU, where he was researching a medieval Jewish poet,
        and I told him I was
perfectly happy writing poetry on the side. He wished me good luck. I never saw
        him again.

I bought *The Art of Love* in hardcover at Papyrus or Salter's as soon as it
        came out,
a few years before our son was born and we left New York because we knew
we would never have enough money for private schools.

The Art of Love reminded me of the Ovid I had read in Israel on the grass
        under open classroom
windows with my head on Nancy Van Haren's lap in 1965. Nance read Gibran.
        Inside they were teaching
Hebrew grammar. *Don't write what you don't want people to know* was advice
        I remember from Ovid.

I wrote an homage to Kenneth Koch's homage to Ovid that Richard
        Brickner, my New School
writing teacher, did not like. Not understanding Kenneth Koch's super
        cool slant on parody,
authenticity, erudition, and fun, Brickner said I should find my own voice.

I bought a Kenneth Koch book called *One Train* on Amazon when
        Amazon was new
and laughed out loud reading how he was a hit with the women in
        Sweden because
he only knew one sentence in Swedish, whose translation was not quite
        inappropriate,

but endearingly bland. "A Time Zone" was about Frank, Larry, Jane,
        John, Boris,
Williams, old Mystery Plays, Harvard, his wife, *Kenyon Review*, Cedar
        Tavern,
de Kooning, John Cage, and Europe helping him discover his own voice.

I read Kenneth Koch's *New Addresses* flying back from my aging mother
        in Laredo, Texas.
I identified Kenneth Koch's allusions for a young Mexican woman who
        had heard me laughing.
We texted for a few weeks after the flight, but I wrote like a know-it-all.

On a visit to Ohio, I met a man who had been in Kenneth Koch's Hebrew
School class. Ironic!
I had just used Kenneth Koch's *Wishes, Lies and Dreams* at a Hebrew
high school.
I asked the man what Kenneth Koch was like as a boy. "Normal, but
always reading poetry."

I once saw Kenneth Koch at my subway stop. I said, "Ken Koch!"
He said, "Do I know you?"

How We Got Our Second Dog, Lucy, February 1, 2003

I was walking home from shul, remembering
how news of the Columbia Space Shuttle crash
had spread through the pews until it reached the rabbi,
who announced it prior to the mourners' *kaddish,*
which he decreed as also for Ilan Ramon.

When I saw Jay's wife, BJ, getting out of her car,
she told me they're planning to give away their new beagle.
One week was enough. "We're just not a dog family,
and it's making Jay pre-asthmatic. Lucy is too hard to train. . . .
If you know any dog people interested—"

"Give me ten minutes," I said. "Sandy's old
and loves when neighbors visit with pups.
She needs an Abishag. And," I added,
"Miriam feels Sandy is Ezra's."

An hour later, with two subdued daughters,
a training cage, three books on beagles,
and a little black leash, Jay delivers Lucy.
Eleven-year-old Miri is thrilled.
Sandy is cautious. Lucy demurs,
then bites furniture.
Leslie cleans up twice the first hour.

Jay tells us everything he's learned
about beagles from books.
I remind him of Bob Goldenberg's joke
about the yeshiva boy who cries with glee

after two hours in the New York Public Library
Reading Room, "Now I know swimming!"
Jay doesn't smile.

He tells us beagles have big ears
to improve their smelling.
He sticks his head forward and down,
shakes it and dangles his hands
to copy beagles' ears.
"It roughs up the grass,
so they can get a better scent."
We promise Sophie and Rachel
they can visit Lucy
any time they want.
As they leave I say to Lucy,
"Say goodbye to your birth parents."

What God Doesn't Understand

Drash: Jocasta, Mother of Oedipus, Reflects in Hell

The seer decreed that someday our son
would kill his father and take me as wife.
He foretold the curse, but not how to resist.
Character determined that.
Never did we hear the seer say,
"Raising him properly will do you no good.
Best have him die trapped like a bear."

What if, I ask now, we had vowed to the world
to save every child cursed by the gods,
to become sanctuary to the tired and poor,
to help the orphaned homeless breathe free?
Then, when our son grew to be a king,
he would know compassion
can be as strong as a plague.

The seer decreed what could not be denied:
Our prince would grow into a beast.
But ordering our newborn baby's death
was unnecessarily cruel defiance. Who knows?
Had we tried to resist with a generous heart
Fate itself might have lost its nerve.

What God Doesn't Understand

God doesn't understand nostalgia
because God is timeless. To God,
what God gave us once is enough.

God doesn't understand addiction
because God gave us all the tools
we need. For the same reason
God doesn't understand adultery,
art, backgammon, or golf.

God doesn't understand peace because
God created us to make the world just.
To God, not fighting for justice
is a surrender to sin. That is why

senators, philosophers, free women, and bards
must unite to teach God a good lesson.

Shul

*A response to Rosh HaShanah Letter from M.W., who
"can't be bothered celebrating any of the Jewish rigmarole anymore."*

You get to sing and learn and eat with others, some of whom lived
    centuries ago or never.
You get to watch kids whose names and birthdays you don't have to remember.

You get to celebrate seasons and new moons and stars that measure
    Sabbath's end,
not just here but all over the world, and you get to help people all over, too.

Your kids get to launch puberty at a party, welcome change, find
    kindness not dread in challenges.
If a loved one dies, you've got people to act like loved ones 'til you pull through,

and when you fall in love forever or decide to act that way, or when you die,
it's less lonely through a shul. Which has little to do with theology

but somehow wouldn't work without it.
What's not to like?

Life Stories

A child, playing in the woods, finds an old man dying.
The old man sits him down and says,

When my grandfather couldn't find a word,
he blamed it on his Latvian birth.
When my father couldn't sleep at night,
he blamed it on his combat years.
When my mother turned to alcohol,
she blamed it on her late divorce.

The child, playing in the woods, is not listening.
Maybe the child is right.

Religious Language

Home-care nurse Yolanda answers,
"*Es Sha**bbat**,*"
when Mother, bewildered,
asks what the candles are for.
Blank stare.

Yolanda repeats louder,
"*Sha**bbat**! Sha**bbat**!*"
Blank stare,
hint of anger.

I intervene: "***Shab**bus.*"
"Oh! ***Shab**bus!*" Mother says.
Yolanda is bewildered. I explain,
"*Hay dos acentos en hebreo,
y la senora entiende con 's' en lugar de 't.'*"

Blank stare.

A Zayde's Rhyme

There may not be a God,
but He listens to my prayer
like a partner in pretending
I'm protected everywhere.

And when He helps, I thank Him,
and when He fails, I sing
until the songs themselves become the shields
against my quivering.

At Seventy-Two I Visit My Father's House

I sleep in, wake up to his voice, eat like a fifteen-year-old.
Mah karah la'yeled sheh diber el kochavim?
What happened to the boy who spoke to stars?

I show him an old Hebrew song I discovered
on the internet last night on the flight down.
Ani rotzeh lachzor el ha'yamim hachi yafim sheli
I want to go back to the prettiest days of my life.

We figure out a colloquial Hebrew idiom in the song
the way he taught me to figure out words from their roots.
Ha'yamim ha'yechefim shel Binyamina, ken!
The barefoot days of Binyamina, yes!

We sing along with Chava Alberstein on my iPhone as if
studying the cantillations for next week's *sedre,* after a *shabbus* nap.
Ani zocher hakol zaram leat, ha'shemesh lo miher.
I remember everything flowed slowly, the sun in no rush.

Deli snack and rugelach for dessert.
Almost time to end the Sabbath.
Anashim amru shalom, chaver haya chaver.
People said "shalom"; a friend was a friend.

From his wife's notebook, I copy the names of his new meds.

Our Father's PTSD

Only one of our father's fifty-four missions
caused him guilty dreams all his life.
He was tasked with bombing a bridge in Italy
but, when he reached the target, saw
a white cross on a building near the bridge.
He hesitated. *It's a hospital!*
By the time he realized it was a Nazi trick,
he had kicked out the bombs too late.

My sister and I always wondered
why, of his fifty-four bombing runs,
this one gave him guilty dreams. After all,
nobody got hurt and he avoided
killing innocent victims.
So, after his ninety-fifth birthday party,
we asked him privately in his study.
He answered with a forced patience
that made us eleven years old:

"How many GIs had to die
taking that bridge that I could've—
should've—wiped out with one click—
if I hadn't been so damn indecisive
or thought for a few impudent seconds
that I knew better than my superiors?"

The Day My Sister Is Born

Israel's sixth Independence Day.
I am nine and my father an old thirty.
He is resting with a Pall Mall
after finally figuring out supper.

He tells me he's now what they call
in Yiddish a rich man:
He can't give his daughter
his son's hand-me-downs.

In that shabby south Jersey garden apartment
with a joyously tired wife recovering
in a Philadelphia hospital,
my father is more serious than I have ever seen.

Until I became a father myself, I believed
that this was the moment he realized
he was never going to move us to Israel.

Between the Buried and Me

Between the buried and me,
there is your fear of being alone
that I try to undo by being alone
with you. There is your body

as real as a dashboard
as raw as the space
of a new missing tooth,
There are grandchildren.

There is the memory of that time
you said, "Porn must be like hypnosis.
You know it's an act, but it works."
There's my father who loved quoting

the way Wellington explained
his victory over Napoleon: Not
that the British were braver,
but that they were braver longer.

There is the summer funeral
of an old friend's brother.
The lasting echo of dry soil
Scattering over the plain pine box.

What Do You Need
Your Money Back For?

All that planning, getting ready,
staying ready for success.
All that reading, clarifying,
then *poof*, end of program.
No refund. What do you need
your money back for, anyway?

I'll tell you this right now,
ladies and gentlemen, if death
didn't exist, comedians would
have invented it.

Dying Man to Night Nurse

He felt what women figure out
on their own, alone, differently,
all over the world

and learn to join or strive to join
with others all their lives
all over the world.

And since he knew he was dying,
he didn't say it nice:
"May I lick you?"

And since she didn't laugh,
he knew it wouldn't be wrong
for him to enjoy, alone,
her serene therapeutic scent.

To G.

I picture you in encounter sessions
improvised by pioneers
in league with savage tribes.
Natives strip you, purge your hustle,
prove rancid character fake.

Pioneers burn shoulders cold,
your mind one organ craving—
after craving, what comes after craving?
"Is this what the Buddha meant by *maya*?"
"Shut up! Don't intellectualize."

At last you hear the certain voice
of poet, wife, and friend:
"Someday you'll write your honest poems;
 learn all you can for now."

How to Die

(For Gil Fagiani)

I sang him the Hebrew psalms
that I had sung my mother on her death bed.

Although his breathing weak, his gums in pain,
when I stopped, he struggled to thank me
with *bravi,* the word I will forever hear him say.

His poems showed how clear detail
can be charged with *bravi;*
his death showed how to die.

Making a Sick Friend Laugh

He smiled
when I told him I was going to chant a psalm.

He shrugged
when I warned him I don't know the tune very well.

When I added,
"That way you'll know you're not in heaven,"

he squeezed my hand.

What God Understands

"One who is unsophisticated should not be asked to confess,
because it may break his spirit and cause him to weep."
    —*The Complete Art Scroll Siddur, 976*

If a death-bed confession might scare the patient,
do not make the offer. The sages explain,
The agony of dying is atonement enough.
If confessing makes dying worse, do not confess.
If confessing makes dying holy, confess.
God grants atonement either way.

What insightful, ancient people
invented this clever, gentle god
brimming with compassion
who wants only that our lives be holy!

I cannot make death painless,
but I can make it guilt-free.
You are forgiven.
The agony of dying
is atonement enough
for the end of opportunities
to make life holy.

In a Hospital Waiting Room

The brain obeys the same laws
that make light move from a star
to the hospital room window
my old high school buddy and I
looked through last night
after his diagnostic procedure.

On TV we watched a show about cuneiform—
all those bills for sheep and property debts!
Somebody thousands of years ago
broke human speech into metaphors
that could be set in soft clay and figured out
long after their language died.

Then we remembered high school math and *pi*.
How hard the teachers must have worked
to make math and science dull.
Mr. Jones's first homework assignment:
Memorize the periodic table.
But Mr. Schwartz did try:
The distance around a perfect circle
will never—even after the end of time—
match up neatly with the distance through.

Maybe the brains that discovered *pi*,
And laws of light, and how to record debt
can help us figure out what's wrong.
And if not, we decided, we should at least find solace
in remembering that *pi* goes on forever.
But then he asked, where? Where does *pi* go on forever?

When Bad
Guys Win

The Night Hillary Lost

Halfway through their Chinese meal,
he asks the owner to identify
the light brown strips
in his shredded beef.
She answers, "After all these years,
now you want to know?"

Driving home, he retracts
something he has just said
because he said it
while his wife was talking.

In spite of his retraction,
his wife can't resist.
"It's just like Donald Trump
cutting off Hillary."

He pulls over,
gives her the keys,
and walks home.

I Dreamed I Fired the Family Photographer Under Trump's Influence

Trump was staying with us 'til the inauguration.
One afternoon when my wife was away,
I fired the photographer that my wife had hired
to take pictures of our grandchildren.
The photographer had exuded warmth
as she showed us glossy photos she had taken
of other people's grandchildren.
I felt she was buttering me up for the bad prints.
I said, "You're fired," and when she said, "What?"
I repeated it, and she turned away and knelt.
I looked at the shivering back of her head,
"She's trying to get my sympathy."

After she left I said to Donald,
"You're a bad influence on me.
I have too weak an ego.
I fired her to please you."
"When your wife gets home I'll explain,"
he said, adding a Latin phrase that I think
he thought means an unbiased observer.
"Remember, I didn't say a thing during
 the entire exchange. I was here the entire time,
and not a word. Did you notice? Did you see that?
When she gets in, I'll tell her."
"No," I said, "that's the very problem.
You're taking over my ego. If you defend me,
then I'm really lost. I must do this myself."
"Fine," he said—and here comes the punchline
that I don't understand but gave me shivers.
He said, "You defend yourself. I won't
be your shield. Those days are *o-v-e-r.*"

A Hora for the First Passover
Under President Trump

It's a chilly afternoon for Tel Aviv,
but we swim like we used to
and shiver and laugh,

because we're not that old,
though I'm fat and bald,
but as soon as I visit you, you—

No! You don't turn me young and thin and hairy again.

Instead, you teach me the Hebrew
for loving a land
even when bad guys win,

for you've shown me the movements
for dancing on sand
with partners you pray to change.

How the Good Republican Caves

I agree it's unfair, but I'm winning.
When I lose, I'll examine my soul.
Let me now praise *Real Life* over *Justice*.
It's Trump who's to blame—I'm just rich.

This time I won't kill any wetbacks,
or belittle some colored man's mind,
and when my women say no, and mean it,
I'll talk about something else.

This land is a breast with one nipple:
malignant, misogynist, mine.
I agree it's unfair, but philanthropy
will help me stay rich and admired.

Western Civ.

We were taught love of country and of God

come from the musical side of our soul—
illogical, perhaps, but as equally needed
as medicine and drilling for oil.

Ignore that truth,
we were taught and taught our kids,
and you walk through life with a limp.

And then we were taught, "Man is born free
and everywhere is in chains."
What we understood to ignore

until we grew up
was that they were praising,
not cursing, the chains.

Prick an American

America is bad on health care because
  Americans never get sick.
America favors the rich in taxes because
  all Americans get rich.
Americans carry guns because
  Americans get bad guys.

America isn't afraid of war because
  Americans never die, and if they do,
they live forever in memorial half-time shows—
    well worth the sacrifice.

Prick an American, he will not bleed.
Prick him again, he re-invents Hollywood.

Frida at the Bronx Botanical Garden

Trotsky's lover and Rivera's wife—
her art on t-shirts and tea cups—
Oscar-winning film about her life
displayed with paparazzi pride;

Children on parents' shoulders,
stuffed into one-stop elevators—
overwhelmed guards and guides
mark the official start of the queue.

Bio-pic about abusive childhood,
disabling, nearly fatal accident,
her love of Mexican flowers
and German father and philandering husband—

On the steps of the Bronx Botanical huge glass hall
local Latino mariachi dancers
sweat to remember the steps their parents
worked hard all their lives to forget.

Inscription

Someday I'll tell my grandchildren
that before I met their grandmother
I had known a poet who had asked me to help
her name the book of poems now in your hands.
I suggested a title from a love poem of hers
I had read in a workshop on the internet.

"Zayde, what's *'internet'*?"

"It's the way people freely shared ideas
before a bad president was elected
who made it only for corporations and the rich.

"Zayde, what's *'elected'*?"

I will explain that, too, and pray to God
they never ask, "Zayde, what's a *'love poem'*?"

Blank Is the New Blank

Hearing aids are the new eyeglasses
Reading is the new rocket science
Explaining is the new insulting
Tattooing is the new ponytail
Obesity is the new smoking
Canada is the new Holland
Mars is the new Moon
Old is the new wrong
History is the Old God

Franklin W. Dixon

I was a newly hired literary agent
meeting with a wizened sub-rights editor
at Grosset & Dunlap.

I had been told to open with small talk.
"I have a sentimental attachment
to this company. In fifth grade we
were assigned to report on our favorite
author. I picked Franklin W. Dixon because
Footprints Under the Window
was my favorite Hardy Boys book. I got an 'A'."

As if reminiscing on Lou Gehrig, the editor said,
"Yes, that was one of our best house names.
I wrote a few of those titles myself."

Let's Make a Deal

I'll sell you the reason that so-and-so died
for a player to be named later .
It will help you help others when they ask,
"Why did so-and-so die? I'd feel better if I knew."
You'll be able to answer, "So-and-so died because
x-3=7y+24w." And people will thank you.
"Thank you. I feel better now. I have closure."

I'll sell you my singing birdcage
for your Mickey Mantle rookie card.
Yes, it sings.
Do you know why the birdcage sings?
It's happy keeping birds against their will.

I'll sell you my self-respect for a malted.
Next time someone goads me with,
"What have you got to lose?"
I won't have anything to lose.

I'll sell you nature for imagination.
All nature knows is repetition.
Maple trees are all alike. Basically.
Sure, they are beautiful miracles,
but boring as hell. Tell you what:
Take the trees, flowers, brooks, fish,
leaves falling on dappled daisies,
even sunsets on the Pacific coast
looked at from a half-mile-high cliff—

Just give me one ounce of imagination,
one ounce, and I'll leave you alone.

I'll Never Be

A Great Poet

I'll Never be a Great Poet

I'll never be a great poet.
I like patterns, but forms make me nervous.
I bend rules like great poets, but not as well.
Whenever I write a poem, I write a different poem.
I'll never be a great poet.

I'll never be a great poet.
Writing love poems makes me ask, For whose country am I a spy?
For everything wise I ever wrote,
I could have written the opposite just as well.
I'll never be a great poet.

I'll never be a great poet.
When my physical therapist sticks her elbow into my calf, I fall in love.
I smile at sad metaphors and don't know plants.
My dog is housebroken but doesn't do tricks.
I'll never be a great poet.

Seven Triolets

1. My Arsonist, My Muse

I forgive you for burning my manuscript;
There's always more where that came from.
Your fire has freed me to leave my crypt.
I forgive you for burning my manuscript.
The idea from the start was to never be gripped
By the past, good or bad a slothful bum.
I forgive you for burning my manuscript.
There's always more where that came from.

2. Contra Dylan Thomas

Why not go gentle into that good night?
Why rage, rage till your family goes mad?
You're wise enough to know dark is right.
Why not go gentle into that good night?
Remind me: what's noble about this fight?
Why make them poor when they want to be sad?
Why not go gentle into that good night?
Why rage, rage till your family goes mad?

3. Immigrant

"You're the greedy old-world reason why such people hate our kind,"
Says the green-card-toting immigrant to others of his tribe.
"No! We're authentic ethnic melons; *you're* a superficial rind!
You're the greedy old-world reason why such people hate our kind."
When there's pressure to assimilate, you're always sure to find
ambition scorned as appetite, a new name seen as a bribe.
"You're the greedy old-world reason why such people hate our kind,"
Says the green card-toting immigrant to others of his tribe.

4. To His Executioners

Knowing now they'll live in dread
Of the moment he's just passed
Turns his fear to joy instead—
Knowing now they'll live in dread.
Night sweats leave him once he's dead,
But in his killers' minds they'll last,
Knowing now they'll live in dread
Of the moment he's just passed.

5. She'll Never Know

She'll never know how much he let her down
He'll never know how good it could have been
Because he chose to play a gentle clown
She'll never know how much he let her down
Fearing the love of an honest frown
He settled for a sympathetic grin
She'll never know how much he let her down
He'll never know how good it could have been.

6. Scent of Her Day

The scent of clean hot melting sand
and sugar in wet clay
floods his lungs 'til they demand
the scent of clean hot melting sand.
Thanks to her he joins the land
of night smells through the day:
The scent of clean hot melting sand
and sugar in wet clay.

7. Unfair Affair

She loved that it was like marriage
He loved that it was not
She no longer wanted to forage

She loved that it was like marriage
He wanted his morning porridge
Each night from a different pot
She loved that it was like marriage
He loved that it was not

Poet's Block

A few days after I start a new poem
I become her willing cuckold.
When I tell my friends she's visiting
her aging aunt in Queens,
they advise confrontation.
How can I tell them that
that would spoil everything?

Instead, I start a new poem.
This one is late for dinner.
She sends me a text.
Her interview is lasting
longer than expected.
You know how these things are,
Sweetie. Just start without me.

a-b-b-a

That's when my buddy, in tears, starts to say,
as the nurse discreetly prepares the meds,
"Nobody *cares*, Zevie. Nobody dreads
your changing the rhyme scheme to **a**-*b*-*b*-**a**.

Creative Hypocrisy

Only when I stub my toe,
read a perfect poem, or sneeze
does what's inside precisely match
what's out.

Other times I conceal and strain
to restrain, refrain, and remain
civilized.
I call this abundant compromise
my last rite of puberty.

What Are Poets Made Of?

Most bodies are sixty percent water,
but the bodies of poets are sixty percent pizza.
There's the Ansel Adams pizza of dunes resembling
the continuity of a loved one's skin, the dogmatic
pizza of *show don't tell* until no one can tell what you mean,
the old-fashioned rhyming pizza of mozzarella
raisins and funny honey, the
tattooed pizza
that announces,
"I'll never
be exactly naked again,"
the veiled misogyny pizza of dirty
words and sports metaphors, the haiku
pizza of air that doesn't have to count.
And the remaining forty percent? Ramen
and scotch. There's the *u r my shrink* scotch
of *today I did this then I felt bad,* the angry young
man ramen that smells of tantrum, only saltier
and sexual, the pedantic scotch of foreign words
and allusions to Ainu gods, and never forget
the Mobius Strip ramen that mystifies as each
loop brings delight back on itself.

Six Differences Between a Joke and a Poem

1. A joke is something your mother couldn't tell;
   a poem is the same thing but with your father.

2. Jokes don't get better the more you hear them.

3. A performer can't misread a poem that she fully understands,
   but the moment she fully understands a joke, she dies.

4. A joke answers, "To get to the other side."
   A poem answers, "To see time fly."

5. Freud never had to write a book called
   Poems and Their Relation to the Unconscious.

6. A joke never waits for you.

I Wish I Had a Mama Who Always Used to Say

If there's a word for it,
it's a cliché.

If youth is all there is to life,
then everyone dies young.

What we know at sixty that we didn't at twenty
is what we will never outgrow.

Sex proves you can love what you do not love;
love proves that sex isn't everything.

Them and Us

They write to prove meaning is overrated.
They write so others will agree
what thugs they have for therapists.

But we write for the cynic who says,
"I could have written that."
Because he couldn't have,

but that he thinks he could
proves that we've pierced his soul
without his knowing.

Leonard Cohen

He did it better, but only better.
He was too much like us to be held in awe.
His songs moved us because we could tell how.

Didn't we all know guys in Hebrew school
who taught girls sex through Buddhist prayer?
Didn't we all devise ambiguities for folk song nights at the Y?

He was not the angry little genius who, each time we heard,
we asked where he came from, surely not Minnesota.
He is not departed or gone.

Cento: The Kind of Poet I Wanted to Be Was the Kind

whose god vomits temple sacrifice,
who sang in his chains like the sea,
who never did too much talkin' anyway,
who turns precious metal into mingled hair.

The kind of poet I wanted to be was the kind
whose world is charged with the grandeur of God,
who asks if he cried who would hear him among the angels,
who retorts, but the second mouse gets the cheese,
whose grave's a fine and private place but none I think do there embrace.

The kind of poet I wanted to be was the kind
whose mother wore black baggy gym skirt pants at YPSL camps before
        she went mad,
who believes his mistress when she says she's made of truth though he
        knows she lies,
who visits his hometown football stadium to watch sons gallop suicidally
        beautiful into each other's bodies—
the kind who outgrows every style he perfects.

How Would
The Truth
Have Helped?

Drash on *The Song of Songs*

Yes, the song is allegory.
The male symbolizes men; the female, women;
the message: sex makes the world holy.

I always admired the stately Tower of David,
clean-shorn lambs rising from streams,
young deer in morning mist, twin fawns.

But when I saw how much you, my love,
resemble them—your neck, your teeth,
your lips and scent—only then

did I understand *K'doshim tihiyu*:
Ye shall be holy.

To Karla

You accepted all the trinkets I bought you with my parents' money for kosher campus food & would place them on the night table next to your paperback copy of *Of Human Bondage* that you read on the subway to & from work, school, second job, & me & you needed to get up early to mold your torso for the art class & that's where I learned the word "torso" & I thought it was only an art word for years. Evenings you would bring home free doughnuts from work & we thought we were ripping off the world & only in New York.

The first time we said goodbye you wore the Madras blouse you had worn the night you told me that you had decided to come to New York for the three-month art project your college required of seniors & whenever I smell damp plaster in a basement I picture your arms carving your torso like a dancer still counting her moves & your very blue eyes & your unsteady fingers writing ideas in your notebook with the novel you were reading a portable desk on the moving train & I am your father's age when he began sculpting bars of soap into busts of New Jersey neighbors who suggested he take art classes at the 92nd Street Y in New York.

The night you confessed your attempted suicide & the night you told me your father had a mistress & the night you read me a new book of poems by John Lennon & the night Margot came home early & did not judge us was all the same night & I thought it was only Margot who let distant cousins use their place for shacking up & a year later when I was in Jerusalem I got your letter clarifying that it was not that I had done x, but that I hadn't done y before x or maybe during, or maybe it was that after doing x, y, & z I forgot to do a & c, though I did do b & did it well, you hastened to add & asked how I had been & told me you had a hard year after you ditched me & I re-read the letter for weeks & lost it & did not look you up when I moved back to New York.

Ellen

You worried that you smelled bad, told me your brother used to call you
      "Stinky,"
but when I think of you in front of me, naked, still alive, I smell sweet
      outdated subway maps.
I taste Good & Plenty, a trace of tooth decay, very slight, and, before the
      chemo, pot.

What made me think of you today, almost fifty years later?
Could it be your proof of God: that men enjoy sex with women?
Could it be the medical marijuana I'm considering for my back?

Or maybe it's the David Brooks piece in today's *New York Times*.
Bonhoeffer, Benedict, and Gerald R. Ford—three ways to fight the new
      president.
Remembering Ginsberg's poems against LBJ and the Blake we read
like a movie script, I thought up a fourth and maybe a fifth.
"The weak in courage is strong in cunning" and
"Always be ready to speak your mind,
and a base man will avoid you."

Love Bird Jam

They sing differently each time
What they play they never play again

They enjoy what they miss the first time
Because they know there will be a second and

Third and hours and anyway what do people
Mean by "miss" or "first" or "again and again"

When there's always time to be wonderfully wasteful
Time to be wonderfully wasteful?

Invitation to a Voyage

I want our love to be a trip abroad
where everybody else knows
which TV programs are silly
and which are simply dull.

Where everybody knows
how to rate a native's smile
and how far to press the vendors.
We don't know any of that.
Nor when to add the garlic,
or the shortest way home by bus.

I want our love to be a trip abroad
where everybody else knows
how to order and get obsequious
when the waiter brings
the chocolate-spread dessert
they were denied as kids.

Where everybody knows when
to break into song at weddings,
and when to stop clapping in unison.
Not us. Clap clap—oops.
Everybody stares. We don't mind.
Everybody says, "Good evening,"
without irony; not like our
"Have a nice day."

In short, I want nothing about us to be
natural, automatic, normal, or real.
I want to start everything with you

in a country that doesn't know the rules
for baseball, or that one must eat
turkey with jam in November.

You Don't See an Accident

Memory is a book that doesn't have to be published
because it hides the way Karla from long ago
nearly drowned the night she whispered to you
We have to break up but didn't mean it you realize
now as her frown surfaces in a slow traffic
daydream on the way to work you wonder
if she regrets her strategy why isn't the traffic
moving? You don't see an accident or know
of a Mets or Yankee game on your way to work
that you can get to with your eyes closed.

The Truck Driver's Wife: A Letter

You're the hair in morning coffee,
greasy wristwatch on a cook,
the banjo-driving vagabond
all cowgirls want to hook.

You're the smile at every barbecue
that's fake, but what the hell?
Once we mingle lust for lust
you fill an empty shell.

You're the gossip of the neighborhood,
the lawn that's mowed too late,
and every spring paired butterflies
mock my dreary fate.

But damn if there's a night of ours
that I don't feel your hand
find something in my flesh that makes
a garden out of sand.

How Would the Truth Have Helped?

She married a man she hardly knew
so her life would be rich with surprise
and she loved like a woman who was sure to the end
that her husband would never find out.

Now each of her lovers remembers her most
for the way she did most of the work.
Her epitaph asks everyone who walks by,
How would the truth have helped?

Valentine's Day Correspondence

Fifty years later she finds him on Facebook:
"Why'd you do me wrong?"

He remembers it all and explains,
"You were too cool for goodbyes.
Electric back-up, powder blue summer boots,
lyrics mistaking bluntness for sincerity—
I felt if I had face-to-face broken up,
you'd have laughed at my little boy take on sex.
In fact, I remember only one time
you ever called me your boyfriend,
and that was indirect."

She remembers—and agrees!
"Yes, when I told you the doctors said
I should tell my *boyfriend* to be less rough.
That's what I found you on FB to tell you about."

After fifty years and therapies, she agrees.
"Those '68 doctors chauvinistically blamed
All my dysfunction on men."
Then she writes of her son, ex-husband,
happy lesbian marriage, and career.

She closes with this:
"If our generation hadn't invented gay pride
and nice-girl bonking, our affair would have been
a taste of marriage for millions."

 He adds, "Bad taste; miserable millions."
They swap pictures for their wives and agree to keep in touch.

Loving to Lose

He loves to lose arguments with his wife:
The parkway would have been faster,
gluten free pasta reduces inflammation.
Dylan didn't deserve it.

To avoid seeming spineless, he puts up a fight,
but as soon as he detects a win,
he reaches for his straw man to beg the question
with a good ol' *post hoc ergo propter hoc*
that he's sure she'll snag him with gusto.

Works every time.
She salivates, pounces on the flaws.
He's ravished, she's happy, they kiss.

Don't Love Me

Don't love me because I'm the best.
When a better comes along, you'll leave.
But tell me I'm the best.

Don't love me just the way I am.
When I change, you'll leave.
But say it's just the way I am.

Don't love me because I love you so
I have no right to waste your time.
But give me all your time.

Interpretation of Dreams

All the fuel tanks in his dreams—
when he's hauling a load of dishes,
client keepsakes, and beds—are about her.

He knows this because when he inserts
the nozzle, the gas seeps over his hand,
drenching his wrists and sleeves

until balloons—white wine balloons—
form along his pants and pop.
And the quesadillas never get cold.

Stage Two

The part of her cheek that got big when she smiled.

The way she chided her husband when he did yoga stretches in public.
Like Israeli wives correcting their husbands' bad English.

The time she wrote the board of directors that she smoked near the pool
because she wanted a socially acceptable way to contort her face in public.

The day she announced to our carpool that she was taking Russian
so she could make cool grunts in the car.

The way her husband would slide into a red neck accent when debating
the school board bus district lines. He had never lived in the South.

All these things told us their marriage had entered Stage Two.

Old Man Jokes and When to Use Them

When your friend repeats what you just said a little bit wrong,
tell the one about the New York nursing home.
Mel to Norman: "I just bought a $20,000 hearing aid."
Norman: "Really? What kind is it?" Mel: "A quarter to seven."

When your Texas nephew takes you out for drinks
to learn what it's like to be seventy-two,
tell the good news/bad news joke.
"You can drink more and bonk longer. You have to."

When you argue over prayer as ritual or as inspiration,
tell the one about the French nursing home.
Pierre to Jacques: "Do you remember all the women you chased?"
Jacques to Pierre: "I remember them all, but I don't remember why."

At Sixty He Remembers 1960

Every soft drink had a slogan
Every cigarette a jingle

Every puff a ritual
Every comb a calling card

Every teacher understood
Every family sacrificed

Every book a consciousness
Every poem a vision test

Every law hypocrisy
Everyone was angry

Every breast was beautiful
Every kiss was holiness

Every car a tune
Every afternoon

Every pill a tool
Every drug a school

Every student tried
Every parent pried

Every play a tour
Every film mature

Every rebel strong
Everyone was wrong

Every hunger wise
Real love the big surprise

A Pat on the Back

I felt so encouraged when Mr. Boyle
put his warm big hand on my shoulder
during my first high school History mid-term exam
that I risked an inference
that I would never have made
without Mr. Boyle's real pat on the back
that every good teacher
willfully, dutifully, innocently, gave
deserving students in 1959.

Notes on Retirement

I am a little girl who just learned that boys don't have periods,
so I prayed to be a boy and it came true.

An attractive strange woman enters my house.
She says, "Just enjoy having me around."

My wife corrects my passport renewal form,
"Your hair is not brown, it's white."

All the neighborhood kids know the name of my dog.

Because
She's Beautiful

What's Wrong with Loving a Woman Just Because She's Beautiful?

It's superficial.
> *Of course it is. Don't beg the question.*

A beautiful woman can be too vain to love back.
> *She'd be right. I'm talking love,*
> *not win–win business deals.*

You're talking sex.
> *I'm talking love:*
> *that word we use*
> *for the feeling we get*
> *for the body we can't live without.*

Beauty is an unfair accident of birth.
> *Unlike what? Religion? Race? Sexual orientation?*
> *The land you'd give your life to defend?*
> *The expensive school your parents could afford?*
> *I ask again: What's wrong with loving a woman*
> *just because she's beautiful, as beautiful as you?*

Let Me Overthink the Ways

Why do I love you? Let me overthink the ways:
because when I was little at the height
of elementary school the budding sight
of girls in curls gave me a taste of grace;

because my mother sought to make my days
a search for ways to shine more light
on things we all knew to be right;
because my father taught with joy to praise

art, words, and thoughts which have no use;
because the paradox of love is found in faith
that real lips turn ideal love loose

of abstract thought, yet real breath
in lovers' sighs can make them choose
a love unreal that knows no death.

Holiday

Old lovers are fallen soldiers
who return like religious holidays
for questioning once a year.

"Have you been watching?" we ask.
"Against the rules," they reply.
"Since when did rules slow you down?"

"Since we died."
"Oh, really? Then explain *this!*"
We slam a dream down on the desk.

The old lovers, sentenced and blindfolded,
are offered famous last words. They cry out,
"We regret thinking only of ourselves."

Overwhelmed with mercy, we argue their defense,
"But you were only 21!"
"We know that," they answer in unison, "but still. . ."

Then, some years you, and some years I,
distribute the Medals of Honor, while the other leaves
orders to shoot them at dawn

and we make love like a pair of new saints.

Anniversary

To her, Time was a beaded necklace,
each bead's stem connected to the next
like the charms children used to win from bubblegum machines.

To him, Time was a deep wide lake
on which an irresistible woman swam in circles
with the cunning of a capricious bubblegum machine.

To neither was time a river, or like anything they'd heard before,
though yesterday she told him Time felt like the overhead fan
whose blades never look the same length from the bed

no matter how many times she fondly recalls the afternoon
when they assembled the fan with blades of equal length.

Sunset, Sunrise

1.

To become as hot as the body I'm with—
that's how good sex always felt.
Only with you it felt wholesome, too.

2.

The way your arm goes through your sleeve.
The blouse you button without looking.
The shoes that every morning match your belt
in the ordinary dawn before breakfast.

Lover's Will

Please promise if I die
you'll find a new man,
show him what we figured out.

It won't be the same.
Why should it?
That's what we figured out.

But love him to keep it going
because I'm in your bones and
love the way you love.

To My Freshly Painted Deck

The directions on the can say *Be consistent. Don't be blotchy.*
After twenty minutes, I dab a spot that I had missed before and dab it again
just to make sure. I'm not being consistent.
I have made a blotch. I plot sections on an imaginary grid.
I shall paint only one section of the grid at a time. Oops,
I see a board I left ten minutes ago that needs a little more paint.
It is out of my current grid.

Should I give it a dab now, or press on in the name of consistency?
I can fix all the little errors at once when I'm done. But then won't
they dry in different shades? And if they dry in the same shade,
how will I find them to fix? Maybe if I can't tell, nobody can?
Well, not right away, but the spots that only get one coat
may wear away sooner than the rest. I muddle through the slats,
splinters, dry bubbles, and holes. I have not become consistent.

Deck! Painting you is like learning a language.
Should I go to future tense before mastering the past?
Absolutely!
I ignore your corrections of my imperfect tense,
Your vestigial forms of dry old paint,
your knots of syntax and agreement.
Will I fix mistakes in the final coat?
Deck, this the final coat.

I still use *ser* for *estar*, and my accent sounds like I'm mocking Mexicans.
But honestly, Deck, it's not a bad job.
How was your weekend? Not bad, I painted my deck. Wow, all we did was....
I visit Italy and figure out some Italian, thanks to the Spanish I failed in school.
In Spain I joke with waiters about Americans' love affair *con "takeaway."*
I know the verbs from the nouns in Cuban songs and can always tell
        when they rhyme.

You are truly beautiful, my imperfect freshly painted somewhat dappled deck!
Let all who disagree ask painters, leaders, and happily married poets.
Let all who disagree ask anyone who speaks a language. Even their own.

Notes

Page 1: "First Visit to In-Laws"

I wrote this poem in 1969 after first meeting my wife's parents. I asked Jay to use his skills as a Hebrew calligrapher to make this into a concrete poem. Jay blended the actual wording of the *ketubah,* the Jewish wedding contract, with my English language poem. Since English reads from left to right, and Hebrew from right to left, the two texts (and mentalities?) face each other in what Jay and I felt was one difficult, achievable poem.

Page 5: "One Month After the Six-Day War"

About a month after the 1967 war, I was stopped in Jerusalem on a major downtown avenue, Ben Yehuda Street, for writing in my notebook at 2:00 a.m. The border patrol thought I might be a terrorist spy taking measurements of Jerusalem's buildings. When I showed them this poem, they apologized and drove away. Since I had spoken to them in Hebrew, I don't know if they understood the English in the notebook. I've often wondered if they had understood the poem and felt prompted to begin a discussion right there in the middle of the night about the proper role of a threatened country when it becomes the conqueror.

Page 8: "Time Machine: A Villanelle for the Jewish Center of Teaneck"

The villanelle is a strict, demanding, old French poetry form consisting of no more nor less than two refrains presented in a specified order, in five stanzas of three lines and climaxing in one stanza of four lines that must end with the two refrain lines. And only two rhymes. In aba order. Each line must have exactly the same number of syllables. I chose this archaic inflexible form as a metaphor for the archaic inflexible nature of the subject of the poem.

Page 9: "Civilization in Three Stanzas"

The melody of "Bella Ciao" comes from either an Italian peasant fishing song or a Jewish wedding (klezmer) melody transmillted via Roma (Gypsies) into a rousing Italian partisan song. See *http://riowang. blogspot .com/ 2008/ 12/bella-ciao.html.*

Page 10: "Israel"

leket, literally "gleanings." According to the bible, the gleanings—the seeds that fall on their own during harvest time—were to be left for the poor. See this law dramatized in the Book of Ruth.

Gush Imunim, one of the first Israeli movements that emerged after the Six-Day War and that believed in Jewish settlement in the conquered territories on the west bank of the Jordan River, which they call after their biblical names, "Judah and Samaria."

biluim, an early Zionist movement that believed in settlement of the ancient homeland of the Jews. The major differences between this settlement group and Gush Imunim would be the subject of an entire book on the history and development of Zionism before and after the founding of the Jewish State in 1948.

sug alef, sug bet, ixtra., "category a, category b, extra." After eggplant is picked it is taken to a conveyor belt in a barn where workers sort the harvest into three categories: Domestic, Keep on Kibbutz, and Export.

sh'ma, the Jewish confession of faith, pledge of allegiance, and statement of faith, the sh'ma is recited daily at two services, at bedtime and on one's deathbed. Just about every Jew in the world knows its first sentence by heart. Hear, O Israel, the Lord is our God, the Lord alone. There are disputes about its translation. The last word "alone" (in Hebrew echad) usually is translated as "one". On good authority I've been told it was used to signify "alone".

Israel the idea was to become normal,/ Israel the idea was to become holy,/ Israel the idea was redemption, the state of Israel is the result of not one but many different competing, Zionist movements. Each one had a different blueprint for what the modern Jewish state should be. Religious? Socialist? Capitalist? A light unto the nations? A normal place for Jews finally to become normal after two thousand years of being different? I try to cover a bunch of them in three or four lines.

sabony, literally, "soapy," the term is Israeli slang pejorative for Americans. Because we're so soft? Because we shower so much? Because many of the people in the last group of Jews who felt assimilation to be a tempting alternative to Jewish identity became soap?

American shoulder to the wheel, many lines in this poem are, as I say in the epigraph and in the poem itself, riffs on Allen Ginsberg's poem, "America." The last lines of his poem are worth quoting verbatim:

I'd better get right down to the job.
It's true I don't want to join the Army or turn lathes in precision parts factories, I'm nearsighted and psychopathic anyway.
America I'm putting my queer shoulder to the wheel.

Page 13: "Al Het"

Jay read this poem in one of the Havurah's early high holiday services on Yom Kippur. I wrote it as an attempt to use the format of the traditional group confessional prayer, "Al Het" ("For the Sin") as a model of individual reflection. It begins with trivial transgressions and then goes too deep, but comes back with personal and collective observations that make it, in my opinion, into more than a simple parody. I reprint it here because, as I re-read it fifty years later, I am struck by the poem's absence of love. It was written in the 1970s.

Bontshe Schweig in Sodom. I. L. Peretz (1852–1915) wrote a short story in 1894 about a humble man named Bontshe Schweig who was greeted in heaven with great fanfare and offered anything he wanted as a reward for being a model of self-effacement on earth. He asked, if it wasn't too much trouble, for a fresh roll with butter every morning. The story is a brilliant touchstone for one's political maturity. Children see—and regrettably are sometimes taught—the story as an example of the delayed rewards for piety in the hereafter, but most of us by adolescence understand the story as a masterpiece of sardonic humor in which Peretz bitterly indicts the passive ghetto mentality for being so emasculated that it can't even imagine a better world—even when the heavens themselves offer us anything we want. *That* is the true meaning of *golus*, exile, diaspora.

Sodom, sinful city of the Hebrew bible.

Page 29: "Shul"

Yiddish for synagogue; **Rosh HaShanah**—Jewish anniversary of the universe's creation, the Jewish New Year.

Page 16: "Religious Language"

There are basically two accents in Modern Hebrew: one used by Jews from Eastern Europe, called Ashkenazi; the other used by Jews from Spain, North Africa, and the Middle East called Sephardi. The big difference is whether the last or the next-to-last syllable gets the stress. Also, one consonant is sounded differently: Sephardi Hebrew says "t" when it sees the Hebrew letter *tav* without a dot in the middle; Ashkenazi Hebrew says "s." Israel speaks Sephardi Hebrew. The Israeli would say "ShaBBAT"; The East European would say "SHABBus." No doubt Yolanda's other Jewish clients spoke Sephardi.

Page 49: "A Hora for the First Passover under President Trump"

The *hora* is the national circle dance of Israel, brought over from Romania in the early years of Zionism. Begun in ancient Greece, the word hora, which derives from the Greek word *khoros*, is cognate to chorus, choreographer, and choir. According to *The Forward*'s Philologos, the Romanian Jewish dancer Baruch Agadati created a hora in 1924 for a show that toured pioneering settlements of the Valley of Jezreel. "Within a short time. . .the hora became a symbol of [pioneers'] capacity for joyousness despite their regime of hard work and ascetic living" *(Forward,* December 2017, https:// forward. com/culture/12226/hora-history-00940/)

Tel Aviv, Israel's first major city founded on a non-biblical site, Tel Aviv symbolizes a purely "Zionist" city. Named after Theodor Herzl's Zionist novel *Altneuland* (Hebrew: *tel* an "archeological mound") *aviv* ("spring"), the city symbolizes a modern Jewish state free of ancient history, archeology, holy sites, biblical allusions.

Page 51: "Western Civ."

The title uses *Civ.* instead of *Civilization* because it alludes to the college course.

Page 54: "Inscription"

Zayde, Yiddish for "grandfather".

Page 73: "Cento: The Kind of Poet I Wanted To Be"

A *cento* (from the Latin word for "patchwork") is a poem in which every line is lifted from another source. This is not an exact cento because I paraphrase most of the allusions, but I so heavily borrow from other works that I feel it should be labeled a cento, lest the reader think I think I made up the images myself.

Page 77: "Drash on The Song of Songs"

This poem is a *drash,* a homily based on a biblical text, sometimes with admittedly stretched connections and quotes shamelessly taken out of context. This was a literary form at the time of the composing of the Talmud and the New Testament, roughly between 100 BCE and 300 CE. I have always felt that modern readers don't get a lot of the darshanists' humor.

Page 78: "To Karla"

The hidden model is Philip Schultz's "For My Father" in his book *Like Wings.* I love his celebration of the ampersand.

Page 84: "The Truck Driver's Wife: A Letter"

The hidden model is Ezra Pound's translation of Li Po / Rihaku's "The River Merchants Wife: A Letter." "Paired butterflies" is the only direct lift;

the rest is a square dance between totally different cultures.

Page 98: "Let Me Overthink the Ways"

The hidden model for this the Elizabeth Barrett Browning poem "How Do I Love Thee," for which I used the same rhyme words as her original.

Page 102: "Lover's Will"

The model is Shakespeare's Sonnet #71, "No longer mourn for me when I am dead. . ." which for years I loved for its nobility, only to learn in graduate school that Shakespeare's overuse of vivid descriptions of death shows that the poet doesn't mean it.

About The Author

Zev Shanken currently teaches English at various colleges in the New York Metropolitan Area. He taught for many years in the New York City school system. In the 1970s he was literary editor of *Response: A Contemporary Jewish Review*. He is co-founder and curator of "Thursdays are for Poetry," a monthly reading series in Teaneck, New Jersey, and is a member of *brevitas*, an on-line poetry group devoted to the short poem.

Mr. Shanken has been awarded two National Endowment for Humanities Summer Fellowships: "The Art of Biblical Narrative" at Northwestern University, and "The Lyric Poetry of Shakespeare, Keats, Whitman, and Yeats at Harvard." His chapbook, *Al Het*, is available from Blue Begonia Press, and his 2016 full-length book of poems, *Memory Tricks* (Full Court Press) is available on Amazon and Barnes & Noble.

The death of friends and the birth of three grandsons in a two-year period spurred Mr. Shanken to produce a second collection of poems that expand on themes introduced in *Memory Tricks*.

Zev lives in Teaneck with his wife, Leslie. They have two grown children.

To Jay

It must have been Shabbat
Because we're wearing white
And you're holding the plastic cups
We used for jugs of cheap Chablis.
It must have been before the kids
Because they would have been in the photograph if they had been.
It must have been more than just to two of us.
I'd guess Lynne Ellenson took the picture because she's not in it.
Yes, we have hair Yes, we are lithe.
No, there are no rainbows,
But we are smiling
And not afraid to touch.

Thank you for the
"Glimpses into then and now
Friendship,
Always friends
Velvet
Verdant"

As ever,

Zev Shanken

CPSIA information can be obtained
at www.ICGtesting.com
Printed in the USA
BVHW031831070219
539751BV00001B/80/P